ARCHAIA

PROUDLY PRESENTS

MOUSE GUARD
LABYRINTH AND OTHER STORIES
A Free Comic Book Day Hardcover Anthology

Featuring
MOUSE GUARD
RUST
LABYRINTH
BOLIVAR
WILL O' THE WISP
FARSCAPE

By
David Petersen
Royden Lepp
Adam Smith
Kyla Vanderklugt
Sean Rubin
Tom Hammock
Megan Hutchison
Ramón K. Pérez
Ian Herring

Los Angeles
2014

DESIGNER | Scott Newman

ASSISTANT EDITOR | Cameron Chittock

EDITOR | Rebecca Taylor

SPECIAL THANKS TO | Comics PRO, the Free Comic Book Day Committee, Brian Henson, Lisa Henson, Jim Formanek, Nicole Goldman, and the entire team at The Jim Henson Company, Jon Adams, Austromar Logistics USA, Regent Publishing Services, all of our comic book shop retail partners, and everyone at Diamond Comic Distributors.

TABLE OF CONTENTS

MOUSE GUARD:

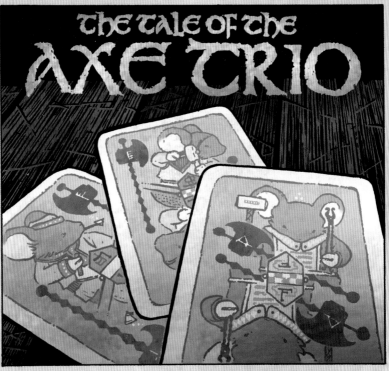

THE TALE OF THE AXE TRIO

STORY & ART BY DAVID PETERSEN

All across the Mouse Territories its residents struggle to prosper amongst harsh weather conditions and predators. A group of selfless, cloaked mice called the Mouse Guard patrol the open country between cities and towns allowing the common mice not just to survive, but to thrive. It takes a mouse of great character to serve in this way, though they often come from humble beginnings...

ORREN, THE FOURTH WIELDER OF THE AXE, HAD HIS TIME WITH IT CUT SHORT. HE DROWNED WHILE TRYING TO EVACUATE THE LAST RESIDENTS IN THE SECOND FLOOD OF NETTLEDOWN.

ORREN

IT IS UNUSUAL FOR THE AXE WIELDER TO HAVE A FAMILY AT ALL, LET ALONE THREE IDENTICAL DAUGHTERS.

THE ORPHANS EXPLORED THE CAVERNOUS BANKS OF THE RIVER TO RECOVER HIM AND THE BLACK AXE AFTER HIS TRAGIC, ALTRUISTIC DEATH.

INSTEAD OF THE AXE PASSING IN ITS TRADITIONAL MEANS, THERE WERE FIVE SEASONS WHERE THE ROLE WAS TAKEN BY THE DAUGHTERS TOGETHER.

THREE ACTING AS ONE.

THEY CRAFTED TWO FORGED AXES, ONE OF HARDWOOD AN. THE OTHER OF A LESSER ORE.

THE MYTH OF THE BLACK AXE WAS WELL KNOWN TO MOUSE AND BEAST ALIKE BY THEN, AND THIS TRIO DID THEIR PART TO BOLSTER THE MYSTERY OF THE CHARACTER.

THE SISTERS WOULD OUTFLANK
A SINGLE BEAST AND CONFUSE IT
INTO THINKING THE BLACK AXE
WAS IN SEVERAL PLACES AT ONCE.

INSTEAD OF STRIKING
THREE BLOWS TOGETHER...

...EACH OF THE THREE SISTERS
HAD THEIR OWN ROLE.

Lynea

THE CLEVEREST DAUGHTER, LYNEA,
WAS A PLANNER AND TACTICIAN
WHO COULD OUTSMART ANY BEAST AND
GIVE PERFECT DIRECTION TO HER SISTERS.

Omaira

THE FIERCEST DAUGHTER, **OMAIRA**, WAS AN INEXHAUSTIBLE FORCE WHO WOULD CHARGE INTO THE JAWS OF ANY PREDATOR JUST TO SLAY IT.

Celandine

SHE WISHED TO BECOME SMARTER OR FIERCER, BUT WAS COMPLETELY CONSUMED WITH THE SAFETY OF HER SISTERS AFTER HAVING ALREADY LOST THEIR FATHER TO HEROICS.

CELANDINE, THE THIRD DAUGHTER, WAS THE MOST CAUTIOUS AND HAD FEARED HERSELF TO BE LESS OF AN ASSET THAN HER TALENTED SISTERS.

CELANDINE HAD A DIFFERENT SORT OF BRAVERY, THOUGH.

INSTEAD OF FOCUSING ON STRIKES AGAINST BEASTS, SHE WOULD DEFLECT THEIR BLOWS WITH THE TRUE AXE.

HER NATURAL REACTION TO CARE AND PROTECT SAVED THE LIVES OF THE TRIO AND COUNTLESS OTHER MICE. HAD SHE TRIED TO FIT IN THE MOLD OF ANOTHER ROLE, SHE'D HAVE FAILED, AND FAILED HER SISTERS IN THE PROCESS.

THE DEFLECTED FOES THEN BECAME EASIER WORK FOR THE PROTECTED LYNEA AND OMAIRA.

THE EN

End.

MAGIC?

TRAGIC.

YOU'RE BETTER OFF WITH US OUT HERE!

KNOCK BANG

THE EN

BACK IN THE DAY, NEW IMMIGRANTS WHO CAME TO AMERICA WOULD SAIL INTO NEW YORK HARBOR PAST THE STATUE OF LIBERTY...
...AND THEY ARRIVED AT ELLIS ISLAND, THE IMMIGRATION INSPECTION STATION.
AND THEY JUST LET YOUR PAREN THROUGH?

FARSCAPE™

"BACKYARD BARBECUE"

STORY & ART BY RAMÓN K PÉREZ • COLOR ASSIST BY IAN HERRING

MORE STORIES.

MOUSE GUARD
by David Petersen

In the world of *Mouse Guard*, mice struggle to live safely and prosper amongst harsh conditions and a host of predators. Thus the Mouse Guard was formed: more than just soldiers, they are guides for common mice looking to journey without confrontation from one village to another. They see to their duty with fearless dedication so that they may not simply exist, but truly live.

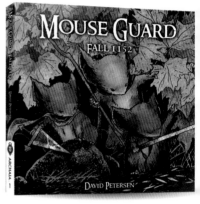

AVAILABLE NOW

MOUSE GUARD: FALL 1152
978-1-932386-57-8 | APR098448 | **$24.95**

MOUSE GUARD: WINTER 1152
978-1-932386-74-5 | MAY090647 | **$24.95**

MOUSE GUARD: THE BLACK AXE
978-1-936393-06-0 | APR130800 | **$24.95**

MOUSE GUARD:
LEGENDS OF THE GUARD VOL. 1
978-1-932386-94-3 | AUG100760 | **$19.95**

MOUSE GUARD:
LEGENDS OF THE GUARD VOL. 2
978-1-936393-26-8 | SEP130878 | **$19.95**

MOUSE GUARD: FALL 1152

ARCHAIA & THE JIM HENSON COMPANY

Archaia is proud to work with The Jim Henson Company to bring the magic of Henson to comics and graphic novels! During our partnership we've released titles from a wide range of properties such as *The Dark Crystal*, *Fraggle Rock*, *Labyrinth*, *The Storyteller* and an adaptation of the lost screenplay written by Jim Henson and his longtime writing partner Jerry Juhl, *Tale of Sand*.

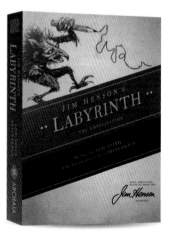

AVAILABLE NOW

THE DARK CRYSTAL: CREATION
MYTHS VOL. 1
978-1-936393-00-8 | SEP110750 | **$19.95**

THE DARK CRYSTAL: CREATION
MYTHS VOL. 2
978-1-936393-80-0 | OCT120755 | **$19.95**

FRAGGLE ROCK VOL. 1
978-1-932386-42-4 | JUN100749 | **$19.95**

FRAGGLE ROCK VOL. 2
978-1-936393-13-8 | FEB110733 | **$19.95**

FRAGGLE ROCK CLASSICS VOL. 1
978-1-936393-22-0 | JUN11029 | **$9.95**

FRAGGLE ROCK CLASSICS VOL. 2
978-1-936393-37-4 | AUG130972 | **$9.95**

LABYRINTH: THE
NOVELIZATION
978-1-60886-416-4 | FEB141067 | **19.99**

THE STORYTELLER
978-1-936393-98-5 | MAY130803 | **$14.95**

JIM HENSON'S TALE OF SAND
978-1-936393-09-1 | JUL110825 | **$29.95**

COMING SOON

THE DARK CRYSTAL: THE
NOVELIZATION
978-1-60886-418-8 | **$19.99**

JIM HENSON'S TALE OF SAND:
THE ILLUSTRATED SCREENPLAY
978-1-60886-440-9 | **$24.99**

LABYRINTH: THE NOVELIZATION

MORE WORLDS.

Explore these and many other titles available from ARCHAIA!

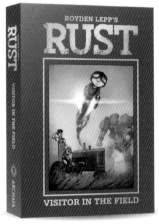

RUST: VISITOR IN THE FIELD

RUST
by Royden Lepp

Young Roman Taylor struggles to keep his family's small farm afloat as the countryside heals from a devastating world war. When a boy with a jet pack, the mysterious Jet Jones, suddenly crash lands into their barn, Roman believes the secrets of Jet's past may be the key to their survival. But are some secrets best left untold?

AVAILABLE NOW

RUST: VISITOR IN THE FIELD
978-1-936393-27-5 | JUL110829 | **$24.95**

RUST: SECRETS OF THE CELL
978-1-936393-58-9 | JUN120795 | **$24.95**

RUST: DEATH OF THE ROCKET BOY
978-1-60886-413-3 | **$24.99**

AN AURORA GRIMEON STORY: WILL O' THE WISP
by Tom Hammock & Megan Hutchison

After her parents' accidental death, young Aurora Grimeon is sent to live with her estranged grandfather on Ossuary Isle, deep in the southern swamps. Joined by her grandfather's pet raccoon Missy, Aurora explores the fog-covered island of graves. When island residents start disappearing, Aurora thrusts herself into the middle of the mystery, uncovering secrets that might be better left buried.

AVAILABLE NOW

AN AURORA GRIMEON STORY:
WILL O' THE WISP
978-1-936393-78-7 | SEP130877 | **$24.95**

AN AURORA GRIMEON STORY:
WILL O' THE WISP

For these and more Archaia titles, go to your local comic book store.
To find the nearest comic book store to you, visit www.comicshoplocator.com.

 /ArchaiaEntertainment   /archaia   archaiaentertainment. **t.**

www.archaia.com | #archaia | #weareboom

THE ESTEEMED CREATORS

DAVID PETERSEN is a three-time Eisner Award winner for his work on his *Mouse Guard* series. He lives in Michigan with his wife, Julia, and their dog, Autumn. You can find out more about David and *Mouse Guard* at *mouseguard.net*.

ROYDEN LEPP was born and raised on the Canadian prairies. He was kicked out of math class for animating in the corner of a text book, and he failed art class for drawing comics instead of following the class curriculum. He now draws comics and works as an animator in the video game industry.

ADAM SMITH started self-publishing comix and zines in Arkansas while still in high school. He lives and writes in Kansas City, Missouri now. *Long Walk To Valhalla* with Matt Fox, which is in production at Archaia, will be his first full length graphic novel.

Since graduating in 2008, KYLA VANDERKLUGT has been working as a freelance illustrator and cartoonist, alongside drawing and self-publishing her own comics. She lives in rural Ontario, Canada, kept company by her dogs and chickens and her many, many books.

SEAN RUBIN writes, illustrates, and designs, all while living in New York City. He is also co-founder of the intrepid MNY Group.

TOM HAMMOCK grew up in Northern California and studied landscape architecture at UC Berkeley. Presently, he lives in Hollywood, where he drinks tea and designs films when he's not writing graphic novels. Tom doesn't have a pet raccoon, but if he did, it would be like Missy.

MEGAN HUTCHISON always knew that she would have to be an artist in order to focus her distractive tendencies towards good and not evil. This led her to attend UCLA as a Design/Media Arts Major and the American Film Institute. You can find Megan illustrating, posting weird sketches on Instagram, and showing at art shows around the Los Angeles area.

RAMÓN K. PÉREZ is an Eisner Award-winning cartoonist and illustrator best known for his graphic novel adaptation of *Jim Henson's Tale Of Sand*. He has also illustrated *Wolverine & the X-Men* for Marvel as well as his creator owned endeavors *Butternutsquash* and *Kukuburi*.

Coming from an illustrative background, IAN HERRING is an Eisner Award-nominated colourist based in Toronto and working out of the RAID studio. He strives to collaborate with artists and writers to help a project reach its maximum potential.